Flowers of the Quantocks

Childhood Memories

Kim Ora Rose

White Flame Publishing

Copyright © 2022 Kim Ora Rose

All rights reserved

The characters and events portrayed in this book are fictitious. Any similarity to real persons, living or dead, is coincidental and not intended by the author.

No part of this book may be reproduced, or stored in a retrieval system, or transmitted in any form or by any means, electronic, mechanical, photocopying, recording, or otherwise, without express written permission of the publisher.

ISBN-13: 9798799623319

Cover design by: Art Painter
Library of Congress Control Number: 2018675309
Printed in the United States of America

To dream a dream
To live a life
Always with love
in your heart
To remember beginnings
Full of love and flowers
To sing the songs of yesterday
With a hand on heart, full of love
As you walk by my side
Each and every day
Two worlds united by a golden thread
To my darling mother
KIM ORA ROSE

Contents

Introduction

Last night I dreamt of Woodlands .... this has been a reoccurring dream all my life, a place of childhood memories where it is always summer. Long days exploring the countryside full of flowers and magic, lost in time itself between the hills, fields down to the Jurassic shoreline of Somerset.

This book takes you through my early childhood with memories and snippets of history about the places I lived in, we moved houses several times in Somerset until we finally settled in the Midlands. We continued to visit our family for the summer holidays for many years and my heart is in those country villages and my love of wildflowers too.

It is a prequel to my Mystical Flower Guardians book that will be published in 2022 this is a book about healing with flowers and spirit guardians. I am a mystic, medium, and channeller who has written a book about flower healing with meditations and a deep connection to each flower's unique spirit guardian.

I hope to enjoy reading about my childhood!

Herein you will find a collection of memories about my childhood and teenage years centered around where I was born in West Somerset. We lived there near my father's place of work and later spend many holidays there with relatives. It is in Somerset that my heart loves to go to, a very special place for me, it was a time of magic and mystery nestled in the heart of the countryside.

There are snippets of historical information, visions of ghosts, and mystical beings that are part of my memories. Also, my love of flowers as you meet them in their natural environments scattered all over the countryside as this book is the prelude to my flower healing book Mystical Flower Guardians about flowers and their spirit guardians.

Entwined between the memories sit my poems and you will sense my love of prose as you meander through my love that sits with each line. Many years ago, I loved to write stories and poems and historical matters, my grandfather used to listen and encourage me for he loved to hear about these things. He was very much part of my life in Somerset and encourages me still, I often see the robin and know that he is near.

This is the land of fae folk, of pixies and dragons, a land between woodland and sea, of magic and mystery.

Since I've started writing I have been remembering that I loved to write as a child, I had such a vivid imagination and as a teenager often wrote poetry, I have found a few poems I wrote about ten years ago and since I pulled all my muses together for the New Dawn poems book I have been remembering more and more about how I loved to write.

As you are reading this, think about your expressions, do you write, sing, sew, draw, paint, craft? What do you love to do? Remember how it feels when you are in flow, with your hobbies, how the light of the universe flows through you. How you light up with Joy. What are you avoiding is it getting your pencils out? Or finding the right colours of thread? Take the time, pick up your pencils, brushes, type your words, sing your song. What is lighting you up right now?

The secret to flowing creativity is to open your doors to your dreams to your own inspiration, stepping through the doorway of unlimited possibilities and letting the ever-flowing joy of creativity flow through you.

It was as if most of my childhood was spent out of doors, in the garden, over the fields, in the woods, wherever I lived it was the outdoors I loved. I have so few memories of the indoor places or the rooms and so many of the outside places. Of flower beds, trees, collecting conkers in the woods and pinecones, pinching pea pods, and trying to boil potatoes in our den.

Lady of the Stream

Down below under the bridge
A tiny pixie all dressed in green
With his striking scarlet cap
Dangling his tiny rod of birch
Into the flowing waters by
With his eyes fixed with focused glare
Into the quiet inky deep pool
All at once, he makes a lurch
Forward, to collect a miniature
Silvery grayling shimmering
Our 'Lady of the stream'

Be still, do not make a sound
For if you do he will surely hear you
Pixies are mischievous you know
They sparkle and dazzle you with
One blow of their corn pixie dust
You will find yourself enchanted

By Kim Ora Rose

Snowfall

It is no surprise that I have no recollection of my first year, but it had been the worst of winters; with blankets of snow and ice, treacherous roads, a season of winter like no other, blizzard and drifts, that never seemed to end. During the coldest winter for 200 years, I was born in late February, the winter to end all winters, remembered as The Big Freeze of 1963. A sensitive mystical child with sun and moon in Pisces arrived into a freezing world of snow and ice. Somehow my mother was able to arrive at the maternity ward, through blizzards and drifts of up to 20 feet of snow, how they managed to travel I do not know, as the villages were often cut off and the narrow country lanes thick with snow. It was freezing cold, with bitter winds, blankets of white covered the whole country and temperatures dropped to minus 20 degrees. There were days of endless heavy snowfall with gales force winds for the north. My father says he had chains on his wheels to help him drive over the deep snow as they do in the Alps; this was the only way to tackle the worst driving conditions he had ever seen. The main road to the power station was kept as clear as possible, as power cuts were often, there were so many shortages of coal that affected other power stations.

My father worked at a nuclear power station at Hinckley Point which didn't suffer the shortages of fuel that the coal-fired power stations had been able to produce more energy their main problem was getting the workforce into work as many roads were cut off. The roads around the power station are relatively narrow and my father remembers it was easier to drive to work when he lived in Stogursey, later in our childhood when we moved to Holford it was not so easy to drive to work.

So, part of my father's journey to work would have been cleared, if you can call it that. Snow upon the snow, ice upon the ice, treacherous journeys that had to be attempted to keep the country that was on its knees with power. Each day my mother set out for the perilous challenge to get food, milk, and supplies from the village, which at times was cut off from the main roads. She was supported by kindly neighbours and the community held together to support each other, sharing food, coal, and other things a reminder of the war years now past.

There I was a new-born babe in arms, beginning my life in a freezing, uncertain world, never knowing when the cold will pass and spring will arrive. One, that loved to be snuggled by a warm fire to feel safe and cared for amidst the chaos of the continuous cold snap and at last, in March the air became warmer, the snowfalls subsided and began the big melting of snow. Spring did finally begin to arrive with the sprouting of plants shooting up through the thawing snow. My father keenly remembers the deep winter, when the cold air arrived just before Christmas and how it lasted and lasted right through to March. It was the coldest winter in his memory since or beforehand, he recalls the snowdrifts and how he had to navigate the roads to get to work and keep the family warm. I have no idea how my family managed during these difficult times, the whole country suffered from low supplies of food, milk, and power. It shows how resilient our parents were during the most difficult of times. When chaos, bitterness hits they carried on, relentless to survive during the most difficult times. So, in the coldest of winters, I was born from two loving hearts.

One day in March people woke up to the first morning without a frost and the warm temperatures began to rise, just like Mother Nature had fired up her own earthly fire and bought the warmth again, like an agreement made between her and the Sun God to restore warmth to our nation again.

My father recalls the effects of the power cuts on time, the clocks in the early 1960s were either wind up or electric, we didn't have very good batteries at this time. So, when there were power cuts this affected the clocks and people would have to regularly alter their clocks to catch up, even when the power was restored the clocks couldn't automatically adjust themselves like ours do now.

Village Life

We lived in Stogursey because my father was an engineer at the Nuclear Power Station at Hinckley Point and this was about 3 miles away. Many of the employees also lived in the local villages many like our family had moved to the sleepy villages nearby far thrown across England, there were rows of new terraced houses for the workers, builders, and engineers, as each village's population expanded the villages awoke to the newness of it all. Change brings change and population growth brings newness too.

During my very early years, we at lived at Church Street in a newly built bungalow, it was spacious, slightly elevated from the road with a good size front garden, long drive, and large rear garden laid to lawn and flower beds. We could see the church from our house as we were on the west side of the church opposite its grounds. The church was Norman and dedicated to St Andrew it dates back to the early 12th century, standing on a corner at the bottom of Church Street turning right on to High Street. The church was originally built as a Benedictine Priory church in 1117. There were several buildings associated with the priory, of a little priory that is east of the church and other priory accommodation. I believe this land was sacred even before the church was built there in a vision I have seen a large standing stone that was situated on this land and it was a place where the pagans would meet for their rituals and ceremonies.

In the churchyard, grounds grow profusely daffodils and these fill the graveyard with their yellow trumpets, they come in Spring with their dancing golden heads, waving in the wind. Yellow flowers are my first love, the first flowers of spring of new life, bright colours and so many spring flowers are yellow. Yellow is the colour of the sun, the colour of happiness, vitality, and joy. The colour of Christ Consciousness rays of golden light too. Daffodils are so full of life, their trumpets heralding the sunshine and golden cups of joy. They bring in the warmth of spring with their promise of the summer sun to come through the turning of the wheel.

When the church was built by William de Falaise it is said to have been built around older features of a sacred building. William De Falaise had connections to the Benedictine priory at Lonlay in Normandy and it was from this connection that a group of monks settle in Stogursey. as part of the St Andrews of the Ards (Black abbey). In those Norman times and until the Priory was dissolved there would have been dedicated gardens full of vegetables to feed the monks and make the cider. The monks always grew their own crops and whilst their diet was very different from ours now; they would tend their crops and gardens. The land is rich higher up on Priory Hill and there is the water supply from Stogursey Brook. There are old stories about the monks being seen on autumn evenings at the time of evensong.

I have always seen or sensed spirit and some of my earliest memories of seeing ghosts or visions from the past were near Stogursey church. I recall telling my grandfather I had seen a man dressed in a habit near the churchyard many years ago, it had frightened me as I could see through him as if not fully there. He was small in stature, head bend as if in deep thought, on the air I could hear the sound of bells ringing. Grandfather loved history and liked to know about the different places around where he lived, he had been born Devon and lived in the County until he moved to Somerset after his wife had died.

This vision has stayed with me for many years. I suppose he was a ghost, and the echo of the distant past or a reminder of the past.

Photo by Kim Ora Rose 2010

Another vision I had in Stogursey was of an angel in my garden, as if a dream, when I was a small child, I saw an angel in white in my garden, it may have been an angel visiting or one of my grandmothers as both were in the spirit in my early childhood. The vision was comforting and showed part of my early mediumship. I was always a very sensitive child who saw and felt everything, I always knew what people were thinking and doing, even behind my back. It had its benefits but downfalls for a child should not really know everything that is going on in an adult's world. I am writing about the church because it feels like an important part of my childhood. Whilst we were never Christians I was baptised but not confirmed.

I was always interested in the church but not fully committed to it either. When I used to visit my grandfather, I would often go to church, there was a natural curiosity to go to church, we when with other children in the village too. If I really thought about I don't think I was drawn to the Church in the way it was presented to me at that time, over years of searching I found God was within me all along and Jesus walks with me every day. This didn't come from being in church but through years of private inner journeying with Jesus and conversations with God.

After years of searching for the truth about religions, I found my peace with God, and Jesus, Mary Magdalene bought me home to the Way of Love and this guides me.

The old priory has long been demolished by the time I was to live in Stogursey but is shown on ordnance survey maps. It is quite possible that the original stonework of the priory has been used in the church, nearby farms, and even in the castle. Originally at that time, Stogursey was called Stoche or Estocha and then Stoke Courcy do and later the name changed to its current name.

Within the walls of the church, there is said to be a Sanctuary Iron Ring, this brings up visions of people begging for Sanctuary at the church from the law. I've heard about this before but it seems quite a romantic idea. It means that if someone was seeking Sanctuary they could ask for 40 days of protection from the church. This was an ancient practice dating back as far as AD 600 up until the 1600s when it was abolished by King James in 1623. So, if you have any ideas about hiding in the church or asking the church for protection, the rules of Sanctuary have long been forgotten. You can hear someone shouting Sanctuary when they are running from the authorities, I feel I might even ask the church to protect me from the Marshalls now if I wish to travel to Somerset to visit the sacred landscape once more.

Photograph by Kim Ora Rose 2010

This churchyard and adjoining new graveyard connect to a small flowing brook that links further up the village to the castle and disappears under the road just by the church and continues on towards the coastline. This is called Stogursey Brook it continues out of the village in the direction of Shurton the next village north. The castle moat is filled by Stogursey Brook water too it is diverted further upstream. Having an affinity with wells, springs, rivers everything to do with water really, as spirit represents water and water is life.

Stogursey is mentioned in the Doomsday book of 1086, it is one of the old villages that lie between the River Parrett and Quantock Hills, where people have lived for centuries. A cluster of old cottages sprinkled around the village with its core buildings of the church, Fore Street, school, and connecting newer housing estates for the farm and power station workers and those that wish to retire to these gentle retreating villages. The Acland Arms public house stood in the middle of the village with the stores, post office, and butchers nearby.

William De Falaise built a fortification in the village which was extended to a small castle with a moat which was built to protect the Somerset coast. The castle was associated with William de

Courcy who was a steward to Henry I and was important to the crown through his powerful connections through marriage. The castle grew over the years and was inherited by Alice de Courcy after there was no son to inherit. It was Alice that welcomed King John there in 1210. After the Courcy families the castle ownership was transferred to the Percy family from Northumberland it had a role in the War of the Roses but after this fell into neglect and ruin. The gatehouse ruin was all that really remained when I was a child, we could see the moat bridge and outer walls and it is the Gatehouse that is now a holiday let.

When I was a child it was in ruins and overgrowth, we used to go for a walk up to the castle and try to sneak into the ruins, but it was covered in weeds and brambles a magical place of knights and queens. So many dreams of make-believe in this old ruin. I remember it being covered in brambles and we often went there to collect the blackberries, there is nothing better than picking your own berries or taking them home to make a blackberry pie. A past time that gave so much pleasure but so rarely done now. Blackberries are a remarkable fruit they are such powerful healing berries full of nutrients and packed with vitamin C, they are fabulous for preserving too into cold remedies, syrups, and jams.

Stogursey Castle is now restored and is a holiday cottage operated by Landmark Trust. When I was visiting the local area with my family about five years ago we visited all our childhood homes and we were very pleasantly surprised to see the castle gatehouse restored. Whilst the village is still small similar to how it was when I was a child there, the Normans had intended it to be a larger town and in the 13th century, there was an inscription 'SIGILL COMMUNE BURRGENSIUM DE STOKES CURCI' on the castle which means Common Seal of the Burgesses of Stoke Courcy. You can see where the modern name came from a combination of the old names Stoke and Courcy, bringing the two words into one name.

On the pathway to the castle there is a small ford with Stogursey

Brook, and on the right-hand side a cottage where there used to be an overshot water wheel this was the village's mill. The brook's source travels towards Stogursey castle across the countryside from near Stogursey Lane, before the claypits. It is joined by a stream from Dodington that flows down to Stogursey too. The water is diverted off to fill the moat of the castle and this must have been put in place over hundred years ago. There are several other streams that flow in and around the village. There is one that originates near Corewell spring that flows to the top West end of the Stogursey near Water farm, this may be Baileys Brook that continues on to Shurton. From the Castle the Stogursey Brook travels down the back of the cottages on Castle .... and comes out near the churchyard, it then goes under the road towards Newnham House at the East end of Shurton, the neighbouring village. Then onward towards the Wick area. There are lots of different brooks that flow down to the coastline and into the marshland areas that are nearer the coast.

Holy Waters

The village has a Holy Well, it is two natural springs, you can find it off an alley from High Street, by the Stone Cross, it was dedicated to St Andrew like the Priory Church and in the past was said to have healing properties. The well was probably a place for Saxon baptisms before being called St Andrew's Well. There are two springs that empty out into a courtyard. We used to visit here often as children with our grandfather, he would bring us here to drink from the springs. I visited this place last time I was visiting Somerset in 2019.

The wells are considered to be sacred from a very long time ago and although they are dedicated to St Andrew. During a journaling meditation in 2018, I was shown a water goddess of the wells and my friend did a channeled drawing of her. She is connected to the ancient stone that I was shown under the church and was part of an old civilization that lived in the local area, a healer, mystic, wise woman, and guardian of the sacred well. I was shown the springs connected to the Goddess Brigid and the triple moon goddess, the water guardian that came forward was very ancient she is called Athe-an, maybe similar to Athena, for her name is very similar, she was a Celt, a water guardian of the ancient waterways that flow from beneath, from the water table and flow out into wells, springs, streams, and rivers. She brings the energy of water priestesses, who tend the flow of life.

The two natural springs each have their own character one is softer better for washing clothes and the other is harder better for healing. In the past, these two springs would have just emerged from the land, in later years a well house was built in the Victorian times and an enclosed courtyard that is still there today. I recall visiting in springtime and the pathways being edged with wild primroses, another beautiful spring flower that reminds me always of visiting the countryside in Somerset. Primroses are likened to the first roses, they come in Springtime and bring the rose energy of ever-unfolding love. Naturally in the hedgerows, they are yellow, a slow gentle hue, harmonizing with their green wide leaves. Other varieties are in many colours that fill our gardens.

St Andrew's Well House, Stogursey

Photograph by Kim Ora Rose 2019

KIM ORA ROSE

Shared Joy

My sister was born the year after me, and for a short while some few months, we moved from the bungalow that overlooked the churchyard to another house in the village. This was a temporary move between our homes, another house purchase had fallen through and we would eventually move to Woodlands, the house beneath the Quantock hills, surrounded by fields of green.

This is the home my heart goes to in the dreams of my childhood, the place I dream of and recall with the fondest of memories. I dream of the stables, pigsties, barns, flower gardens, I often dream of being there once more....

Woodlands

Last night I dreamt of Woodlands,
living there once more, as a child,
with faery folk dancing at the door,
I heard them singing in the stables
Them dancing on the upturned tables
I heard them singing around the apple trees
Wassailing in the orchard
I saw them running in out of the sty
Weaving golden thread in the air
Whispers of gossamer silk
They came and drank sweet tea with me
On mother's greenest lawn
We dined on rose petals and dandelion flowers
Rosehips and candy cotton.
Last night I dreamt of woodlands.......

By Kim Ora Rose

Gate to Woodlands cottage
Photograph my Kim Ora Rose

When I was about four years old we moved from Stogursey to live near the village of Holford we didn't live in the village but outside surrounded by fields but there was a footpath across the fields to the village. It is a small village just on the edge of the Quantock hills and has a pub, hotel some houses, shops, and a lovely quaint church dedicated to Saint Mary the Virgin. It is here I had my first meeting the Mother Mary, my first spiritual as a child, my grandfather took us over the fields to explore the nearby village, we would collect ice creams and visit the shops and the church.

Before we had moved in at Woodlands Cottages, one of the other owners used to look after the churchyard gardens, cutting the grass and tending the rose bushes.   The Reverend liked to keep the gardens clear and tidy and welcomed labour from the local community. Woodlands Cottages were a pair of cottages attached to Woodlands farm, we lived at one end and another couple at the other end. The farm was quite close by I remember going to play in their garden and with their dogs whilst my Mum chatted to the lady that lived there. There has been a farm there for centuries, back in Tudor times the farmhouse had two floors with lots of outbuildings including an "Apple House" a link to the orchards on the farm at this time. I remember the Apple Orchards there too. At Woodlands we had a huge garden and outbuildings, we were forever running around the stables, hiding in the pig sty and in the orchards.

The house was at the end of a narrow lane off Corewell Lane, in the tiniest of villages there is Corewell, at the other end of our home, and there is a spring there and well. There are steps down to the well which is enclosed on three of its sides and a roof-like arch over it. People would have gone to collect water from this well for centuries before plumbing and running water was installed. The villagers say it was reliable and never ran dry. This is little well, or spring could easily be missed it's tucked away but we used to walk up to Corewell to catch the school bus and would seek out everything of interest on your route to and fro.

We lived in an old cottage, miles from the main towns and dwelling places, in a magical place, we were surrounded by the greenness of fields. In a veil or realm of its own light; guided by nature herself with each waking breath, she called me, out into the garden, up the path, over the stile, into the tapestry of ever-changing colours. Within, in my own magical kingdom, my own personal realms are full of flowers and fairies. My heart holds the memories so dear of those early years at Woodlands, drenched in the early mists, with winged friends, robin, hawk, majestic butterflies, and industrious bees. I often heard my name on the wind, on the air as if whispered to by the spiritual realms. The magpies' calls, the dove coos, and my heart sing.

This is where my early life began, on the landscape loved by romantic poets and gentlefolk; between fields of golden corn, barley bedded in redden earth, following tractor lines to the seashore, met by pebbles and mud. That gave way to ancient oak stumps with the high tide retreats that remind us of another time, an echo etched within the landscape. Continue down the shoreline, to the towers of power, looming pillars that blemish the skyline, as they silhouette against the grey of sea merging with windswept shores.

The Elder Tree

Faeries with their iridescent wings
Fluttering around each flower in bloom
Oberon calls to thee
Come to the wild gardens
Come dance with me
Queen Elder ways her wand
Magic and stardust are all around
Golden magic in the air and on the ground
Listen carefully to hear
Faerie music from cowbells
Tingle, tingle, tingle
Dingle, lingle,
Dingle, lingle, lie

By Kim Ora Rose

Daydreams

Between the town of Bridgwater that strides the River Parrett on its journey west to the Bristol Channel and the main route to Minehead a popular seaside town further along the coast, just before the Exmoor hills abide, was our cottage. It was one of three built in the traditional Somerset style with rendered walls and brick coloured tiles. The dwelling set to the side of the farmhouse, near the antiquated village of Holford. The village has only a small population and even less when we lived there, there is a church, Holford Glen which used to be the home of the Huguenot silk factory.

It's an old village and the village just above it, is Dowesborough and iron age hill fort which was previously called Danesborough. The village's name came from it originally being clustered around the "Old Coach Road" where it dipped to a ford in the stream. The stream was in a narrow valley, called Hole or Combe, creating the name "Holeford". Not far from the village is Alftoxton Hotel this was originally a country house and it is where William Wordsworth and his sister Dorothy lived for a year between 1798/9. As you walk around the village you will find the bridge over Holford Glen where two streams met, one coming from Holford Combe and the other from Hodders Combe this is where the wild bluebells grow in their droves and the area is filled with fairy folk they protect this area. It was around this Glen area that the Huguenots settled and began their silk weaving factory. It is hard to imagine that in this small village a family from France settled and started their weaving business, they were said to have arrived in the 16th century after being persecuted in France where they stayed to begin their weaving. The factory sources silk from

Over Stowey where silkworms were hatched and another raw silk was imported unto the French Revolution and then the factory diversified.

Holford is a small village of a few houses that sits below the old "Coach Road" up onto the Quantock Hills. The hills are full of wildness, peace, and wonder they span some thirty-eight miles of the combe, heathland, and shorelines. They are an Area of Outstanding Natural Beauty, nestled between farms and villages, narrow lanes, and streams. The area was recognised in 1956 as being precious and an ancient land full of history and heritage. Up over the "Coach Road" takes you up onto the heath, fauna, flora, bronzed bracken, purple heathers, windswept moors, and wooded valleys. So much of the Quantock Hills is heathland covered with maritime heath, bell-type heather, gorse, and ling that create wild textures and colours all year round.

The delightful whortleberries make the most delicious jams they are similar to blueberries. Where the heather resides, lay the non-native rhododendron shrubs that spread far and wide. Every changing season brings new colours and textures to these ever-changing hills.

Holford was an interesting place it is where Samuel Taylor Coleridge and William Wordsworth lived there very close by when they wrote Kubla Khan. Samuel Taylor Coleridge lived later at Nether Stowey another nearby village and you can visit his house as it is owned by the Natural Trust. The film about the life of Coleridge and Wordsworth was shot in Holford and on the Quantock Hills near Taunton in Somerset. We recently watched the film about Coleridge and Wordsworth and even though the quality of the film was poor we thoroughly enjoyed seeing the beach at Kilve and them walking over the Quantocks, the film is called Pandemonium made in 2001 by the BBC.

The church at Holford is quite modest, with its red sandstone blocks, (probably from Triscombe quarry) its north square tower with its porch that was restored in the 19th century. There has been a church on this land since the 1200s, but this one that is there today and when I was there as a child was built in the 1500s. The tower has bells that are regularly rung. I cannot recall if I remember them as a child. The slated roof leads rainwater down to the gutters that gush when the rain is heavy, you can hear it splashing in the drains. The Churchyard is modest too, drowning out light, under its heavy branches of the yew, it shades the graves with its heavy evergreen needles.

It's always lovely to visit the church, I find the graves comforting, always have, strange really some people are frightened of them when I've always been the reverse. So, one sunny day in the late 1960s, I was out walking with my grandfather in the village, we visited the church and I was playing hide and seek. I ran off into the church and was playing hide and seek with my younger sister. I recall being at the altar end of the church near the lady's chapel, I was tiptoeing on the stone floor, trying not to be heard when I heard a soft voice call my name, and spun round to see who it was.

Before me, was a lady with the softest eyes and she held out a flower to give to me, being I child I took it and didn't really think about it, she said the words to me " all will be well" and whilst I had no idea what she meant at that time now I feel it was comforting for many things changed in our lives during the next few years. I always remember her eyes, they were so dark, deep, and comforting and her voice was so soft but reassuring. She pointed up to the cross with Jesus on the crucifixion and repeated "All will be Well" and these words have been said to me since that time. I am sure looking back that this was Mary, this vision has stayed in my memory for so long. Her loving eyes and soft voice were an old memory of hope.

"All will be well"
"All will be well"

Mother Mary

A field and orchard separated us from the heart of the village and onward west is the village of Kilve that leads to the Jurassic shore, where ammonites are hidden in rigid limestone, shales layer upon layer.

A gentle reminder of ancient life that lived on these shores some eons ago. We were so spoilt there nestled in the countryside, where we could go up on the heath or down to the coast or just be in the fields next to our home. I have so many memories of playing in the field, through the wildflowers, buttercups, daisies, and even of the thistles. Stinging my ankles and pricking my fingers. It was like living in a magical fairy realm, we had a large garden and grounds and every corner of our realm was filled with the wonder of nature.

There are so many apple and pear orchards around this part of Somerset, most of the farms and public houses would have had their own cider press in the past, cider was the drink of the local people, similarly to how small beer was the drink in other places. People would drink cider instead of water in a milder version, its the home of Scrumpy cider too a rough, stronger cider.

There were orchards at Woodlands farm and many more in the surrounding area, apples are a very healing fruit I remember the old rhyme "An apple a day keeps the doctor away" and apple juice, apple cider and apples were used due to their many healing properties.

It was the Romans that learn how to ferment apple juice to make a pleasant drink and years later Normans would grow orchards in France and this became more common place in England too. When they Normans came to Britian in the 11th century they bought their love of cider with them too. The soil in the Somerset was similar to that in Northern France and was perfect for growing apples. Alot of farms would have their own orchards and would make their own cider for their farm labourers to drink especially at harvest time as its a freshing drink for the hot summer sun.

Memories of Holford

Under the shadow of the Quantock hills
Upon the land that sits between time itself,
lie the gentle quiet country hamlets
in their peaceful wilderness,
Lost in time itself.

By the ancient mills
Between the timeless cottages and trees
On a May morn, dost see
Amidst the pungent tiny white flowers
And vibrant bluebells
Blowing on the morning breeze
High on the beech boughs
Sing and squark majestic rooks

By Kim Ora Rose

Flowers in every colour and season, wild birds, insects, and animals all in tune with the turning of the wheel. It is in the garden and the surrounding fields and woodlands that the fairies lived, as a child I would see them and play with them, dancing around the fields, running and having tea parties with my dolls, and always inviting the fae-folk too. They were my companions, they made my life whole, each flower having its own special fairy, I loved the buttercup and daisy fairies, the rose fairies, and many more. I used to make up stories about them and talk to them about my dreams and hopes.

Wild Marshlands

On and on to the turn of the coast to meet the River Parret, where lay feral marshlands filled with bittern, great white egret stalk, shelduck in there hundred and on high marsh harrier fly. The waterways branch out like veins, forever, moving inland, sometimes flooded, sometimes filled with shadowy lagoons, often just a trickle of freshwater reaching out to the salty sea. Ever-changing with each tide, mighty storm, or changing season as with life itself, ever-flowing, ever-shifting, from spring to summer to winter and back again. As is the power of nature, the power to transform her streams and waterways into lakes and flowing streams across the countryside from South of Combwich to the Bristol Channel a beautiful wild place always in flux. A place of beauty, of flora and fauna, wildlife habitats to many birds and mammals, shielding the inland villages and homes.

Here where the mudflats reach out to the pasture there is a rustic path now a haven for bird watchers and hikers. Tall willow trees stretch out over the streams, hawthorns frame the pastures that in the spring are filled with golden buttercups, blue cornflowers, and daisies. Along the hedgerows grow wild roses in softest pink against the thorn blossom in late spring. Around the lazy lagoons, you'll find wild blue irises and water lilies along the still waters. Looking closely, you might see the bluest of butterflies' flutter by on the eastern wind amidst the long grasses, grazing on leaf she dances merrily merging the cornflowers. On a summer's day, the air is filled with a salty breeze, with dragonflies and damselflies shimmering their dainty wings.

Sweet Emmeline Egret

The great egret often calls to me, on the wind, on the breeze
She calls her sweet name "Emmeline" over the marshlands
Upright she stands by shallow waters,
Precise in her pose, ever still, ever tall,
All at once, motionlessly,
she pounces on her prey

Tides ebb and flow over marshy waterways
carelessly throughout the day
She stalks the shallow waters until the dusky sky
With golden plumes she takes flight
Calling out her sweet name Emmeline once more
Homeward bound to her reeded nest

By Kim Ora Rose

For several weeks since I started writing this book, I have been visited by a heron, I saw one from my bedroom window and often see one on the riverbanks, they seem to come more and more and this poem was inspired by the Egrets, a form of heron that lives in the marshlands at Steart Peninsula.

Symbolically the heron asks us to be patient like they are when stalking out their prey, they stand so still watching, then take flight.

They bring their natural energy of tranquillity and stillness; they have great determination too and they bring the message of never giving up. If you see a heron or similar bird remember their message of peace and calm, be still, don't give up your time will come.

The marshlands of Steart Peninsula frame the land, like the River Parret snakes and turns from Bridgwater down to Combwich and into the Bristol Channel, around the land to the West of the river, are filled with marshlands, natural waterways that ebb and flow from the ever-changing tide and freshwater flows between the network of streams and brooks.

Love of Horses

My mother loved horses and she loved to take us up on to the moor to seek out horses and ponies, her father kept horses from time to time, they were so much part of his childhood and early working career. There are family stories of him riding a horse to market at Market Drayton over 30 miles from his home to sell a horse for his father. They would break them themselves and then sell them for an additional income from their bakery business. My mother loved to ride too, she loved horses all her life, we never owned any, but my brother does he continues the tradition of loving horses. I used to ride in my teens and early twenties, this is something I've been meaning to get back into again.

Many of you reading this will share with the love of horses, in the past, they were a form of transport, they are so graceful, we have lost that way of living. Horses are very spiritual and you may have them come to you in meditations, I have a white horse I call *Estella* that comes to me, she is gray and so graceful, I sense you have horse energies that come to you too. You can always trust someone that loves horses, just received that from my grandfather in spirit. He says look at how someone treats their animals and you have the measure of them. There you go messages from heaven to share....

Horses
Photograph by Kim Ora Rose 2012

Triscombe Treasures

My grandfather's second cousin Betty, who we called Aunty Betty lived on the other side of the Quantock Hills in a small village called Triscombe, she lived there with her husband Charlie opposite the Triscombe Nurseries, she worked there tending the flowers and her own garden was such a delight, full of magical wonder, a wild garden if ever there was one, something like a secret garden, where every type of flower and shrub grew in contentment and disarray. Amongst the flowers, there were more plants, and such was their wonderful garden like a secret garden in fictional books. She was so proud of all the flowers all growing together and would delight to show her precious blooms. They lived an idyllic life in the rural hillside, you could walk from their house, up the hill, over the fields up onto the hillside to look up to the skies. She had a field full of sheep too there are so many fond memories of running with the lambs in spring. Aunty Betty was involved with the local church and she was responsible for our Christian upbringing, she would also quote the scriptures to us and remind us of Lent and other Christian festivals and as I write I can see the shepherd within your fields of love and light.

Over lighting her world, he was her constant guide and watched over their bonny lives.

She brings us a message of Lent to us now " *Matthew 6:21 For where your treasure is, there your heart will be also.*" she brings us this reminder of what our treasure is, it can be our connection to God, to Jesus, it can be our deepest connection to ourselves. To our own heart, to your own heart, and what a treasure that is. So, in the days leading up to Easter, in the days of Lent, allow yourself to fully feel your own treasure, your spirit inside and that is where your heart is. This relates to any day, any season, any time with the year, and she is reminding me that at any time in your life. There is a treasure and it is your heart. Step into your heart now and feel all that you have, all the treasure that is within you right now, each and every time you seek your heart it is there. I've just been given a golden ray of light to sense within your heart of hearts, yours and mine, your friends and family, and everyone you know and don't know. She is bringing this ray of light her faith was so strong and she sends the Christed light to you all to share and shine throughout the world.

You cannot contain all this light for it needs to shine and she is bringing this reminder to you and to me today. Not far from Aunty Betty's house there is a standing stone called "Triscombe Stone" is means a meeting place and it feels so sacred there, a place for communities, lovers, and traders to meet in a time not long ago. It is hard to find now you have to travel down the narrow Somerset roads where only one car can pass, up winding roads, or via the quarry roads. The Triscombe quarry has now closed down and is inhabited by wild cyclists and walkers over the purple and bronze bracken paths. I see visions of lovers meeting at Triscombe Stone in secret ronde ques like in Romeo and Juliet, lovers from different families meeting there on the Quantocks, in the bracken to plan their elopement. I am sure Wordsworth and Coleridge travelled over these paths and channelled those famous words of love and prose; with their love of nature, Gaia, Mother Earth and the power of the elements and life itself in all its wonder and mystical.

Even though we left Somerset to live in the Midlands we used to visit my grandfather who continued to live in Stogursey for many years and my mothers' sister moved to live at Nether Stowey which is a stone's throw away. We would call on Aunty Betty and Uncle Charlie when visiting the local areas, which we did quite often until my early twenties. I remember my mother having a fondest for them and I am pausing here to call in, open up to that memory and where it sits, my mother had bouts of depression when we were children, I am hearing, remembering that Aunty Betty was a great friend and comfort to her at these times. Visions of memories of going up to Aunty Betty's house and she and mum chatting helped her. Also, of her coming to our home and helping in the garden, giving advice on the flowers, I can see them now in the garden planting the flower beds and Aunty Betty coming over from the Triscombe Nurseries with flowers, arms full of floral treasures. Wow as you go back to find these snippets of forgotten for never lost memories. She is bringing Lavender she is saying you must have lavender Ann, I can hear her voice now, she is bringing several lavender plant pots, she says you can never have enough Lavender. Here it is, in my long-term memory but she is so right, I love lavender. She is so right, you can never have enough lavender in your garden, the wildlife loves them too.

Aunty Betty is here so clearly on this February day, whilst I write, what a delight, I can see her in her plaits they were always so neatly presented, she must have had the longest of hair, she wrapped them around and pinned them tight. I had a child-like curiosity about what she looked like with her hair down at night. She is bringing me another memory now, a vision of buttercups, she is leading us three, probably my brother in his pram around the field of buttercups, maybe giving my mother a break for a little while, I am dancing, smelling the buttercups with my sister by my side, she is smiling and that feels so right. We do a lap of the field all the way around, pausing to look at the brambles, peer through the spaces in the hedges, to see the cows on the other side. Look down the rabbit holes and have not a care in the world. Aunty Betty squeezes my hand, I feel it now, as if I am there, with her in that field of Buttercups, a summers day, slight breeze, a short walk that seems like a lifetime away, over 50 years ago, a walk in the buttercup fields with a favourite Aunt.

Uncle Charlie was a real character he used to tinker with car engines and used to attend race meets in the past, he had a love of speed and adrenalin whilst Aunty Betty loved to bake and tend her garden. They were never very much into housework or throwing anything away, we would always be offered a chipped china cup and step over the old mantle in the driveway, but they were quite magical and eccentric to the hilt. My favourite flowers from their garden are the ever-fragrant lavender shrubs that decorated their lawn space, some young, some woody reminding me of the triple goddess of all cycles of love and life.

I see them now just a few steps from their garden they had a little meadow of their own, they kept sheep in it at times, we climb over the fence and run and play in the grassy meadow. Aunty Betty used to walk up here and look out over her own little meadow it was a real joy of hers. I think of her as I write and remember, her and Uncle Charlie they were so much part of our early life and I miss them now but know that they are only a thought away. This message is for you, dig out your photos, remember the people from your yesteryear. They are so close and you only have to open your heart and they will bring their love to you, today and every day.

In a time of throw away
nothing meant to last,
memories hold so much
that is part of my childhood past.
Step back in time
To olden days
See what was precious
No matter when past

Kim Ora Rose

Into the fields with buttercups
Galore
Chasing butterflies
Chasing cows
and pausing
to catch one's breath
listening to the robin's
song
What bliss!

by Kim Ora Rose

The village of Triscombe is close to Crowcombe and West Bagborough, these small country villages are situated over the ridge or the Quantock hills, you can reach them via the "old Coach Road" or from Over Stowey, or the long way round following the main road West and turning in towards Taunton. Crowcombe was closest to Aunty Betty's house and its a quaint sleepy village. Aunty Betty along with her Mother Ellen and Aunt Francis all went to the Women's Institue, they would go to the one at Crowcombe, it was started in 1918. These three ladies would go to all the events and those at the church too. They were keen gardeners and would enter the local garden competitons growing flowers and vegetables. Aunty Betty used to make jams and would often bring us some, I remember her strawberry jam, she had grown the berries in her garden too so they were extra special. They would also be invited to the events at Crowcombe Court for garden parties etc.

DREAM

Sea Dragons

Not far along the Minehead road is the village of Kilve, we used to visit on weekends with my parents, it's a fascinating beach full of fossils and ancient things. Kilve beach is within the Blue Anchor Bay to Steart Peninsula SSI protected area and is one of the beaches where you might find fossils, the beach is layered in rocks and stones, there are some rock pools when the tide is out too.

My uncle used to play cricket for the village team and I remember going with my Aunty to watch the match or make teas for the players. Cricket is a peaceful game and pleasant to watch on a summer's day.

It is the home of the legendary *Blue Ben Dragon* who was said to have lived in the shale caves along the coast of Somerset.

He was regularly seen swimming in the sea to cool himself off, after breathing fire. He had been worried about getting stuck in the mudflats on this way into the sea, so built himself a huge limestone causeway for his safe return between land and sea. The Devil had been discovered Blue Ben's lair, he captured him and kept him to ride over the land and sea. One day Blue Ben escaped but in his hurry to get back to his lair, he forgot about the mudflats and fell into the mire, he struggled and struggled to no avail and succumbed to death so close to shore.

In the 19th century whilst some of the blue lias shale was being quarried at Kilve they found the skull of an Ichthyosaur and they named it Blue Ben. The skull is on display locally.

This stretch of shoreline has many secrets embedded in its ancient rocks, memories of ancients that walked and swam over the land and sea. Coleridge spoke about the Ancient Mariner and I feel what about the ancient sea dragons that swam, hunted and lived on these shores. The many sea dragons that fossils lie between the layers of mud and shale, and every now and then, one is found by animals or humans, they sea bed gives up its treasures one by one.

One of my ancestors on my grandfathers' maternal side was related to the British geologist William Pengelly who was born in 1812 at East Looe, Cornwall he was related to my Great Grandma Florence Pengelley. During William's he first went to sea with his fathers ship and later moved to Torquay in Devon. He was fascinated by fossil fish, flints and bones that he had found around his home at Looe. He found many fossils and bones and also excavated Kents Cavern at Torquay. I sure he would have loved to have explored the North coastline in Somerset and would have marvelled at the fossils that have been found there.

There was another ichthyosaur found near Glastonbury that is at Wells Museum these wonderful dragons or dinosaurs lived during the Jurassic period around 200 million years ago. The sea was warmer and came inland not from Street, outside of Glastonbury and this was an important area for sea dragon skeletons. The ichthyosaurs lived on earth for about 100 million years and they were air-breathing, fast swimmer sea reptiles and often called Jurassic Sea Dragons. They would hunt in the waters and come up for air a little different from our view of dragons, who we imagine lived on the land.

Another dragon was found on Stolford beach by some dog walkers in 2019, they found another ichthyosaur and this is on display at Taunton Museum. Also just recently a huge fossil has been found at Rutland Water, in Leicestership.

Strangely when I was on a retreat in Glastonbury I saw a vision of a blue dragon and a white dragon and they are often in my spiritual visions. My sister has written a series of children's books about a little boy and his dragon called George. I love to think how we have been influenced by the landscape of our childhood, and its ancient past dragons that lived by the ancient shores.

Several years ago I visited the North Somerset coastline at the end of a holiday in Devon, we were with the children and had been to Exeter and Crediton to find the places where my ancestors had lived. On our way back to the Midlands we came back via Lynton and Lynmouth and on the main road to Bridgwater, we stopped off at Kilve and stayed at the Chantry Tea Rooms and Bed and Breakfast. We enjoyed some time on the beach looking for fossils and had many walks around the area. When I met the B&B owner it was noted that I had been to school with her brother for a short time and we made that immediate connection.

We explored the Coleridge and Wordsworth Walk upon the Quantocks over the paths of the old groves, it was absolutely fabulous and the views were amazing all over the shoreline, of the power station, the moors, and countryside.

Sometimes when you walk in the wild places it's like you step through a portal into another time and space. We were out quite late on the walk and it was so magical up in the heathers with the ponies and kestrels. This was a time before mobile phones so I don't have any photos from this walk but it remains in my memory. I have such a fondness for the Quantocks of the walks, high above the trees, the heather, and the ponies.

There are myths of ghosts and beasts on the Quantock moors, I have only memories of happiness, picnics, and walks. I know there is a white lady up there that I may write about in the future, she has a sad tale to tell of abandonment and mystery. I met her in my dream state several years ago.

Ancient Forests

To the East of the power station, there is the small beach of Stolfold and this has the Jurassic shale, rocks, and pebbles rocks alongside the other beaches along this stretch of the coastline. It also has the memory of an ancient forest that may have spread out into the Bristol Channel many eons ago. At low tide, you can see the old stumps in the muddy sand, they date back to the remains of a submerged forest some 2500-5000 bc years ago. This forest would have been in the Bronze Age, which shows how very different this coastline would have been in the ancient past. With its remnants of stumps sprouting out of the sand, giving us the imagery of long-lost times. They hint at the past in a way we don't often see, link us to myths and legends of time once lived. We have all heard the stories of great floods and when you see these stumps at low tide they can conjure up all times of mystical stories. When the tide comes in they are hidden once more, to be revealed at low tide again. Submerged forests give us a glimpse of the past, they invite our imagination to dream up what life was like in the Bronze Age. Flints and evidence from people living in the ancient past have been found at Stolford and the nearby Hinckley Point beach, there was a bronze age hoard found at Wick Park near Stogursey and there is the Pixie Mound near Hinckley Point too.

When visiting our grandfather in the school holidays we used to go out most of the daytime; with the local children, roaming country lanes, over fields, seeking adventures. It was only a few miles walk to the beach, across the fields, minding the crops, walking around the furrows, under barbed wire and over gates. We would examine the rocks to find fossils and interesting stones, run on the sand, and peer in rock pools for crabs and shrimps.

My sister remembers going to the beach it was such an adventure, we were left to our adventures out with the local children who knew the paths and interesting places to go. I remember going out all day with our snacks to come home to tea with grandpa. I was often in a daydream, imagining all sorts of things, living in a different realm, times, and having wonderful adventures.

Walking and roaming all day long in the summer sun, we would walk all along the footpaths and coast paths along the shoreline as far as you can go in one day, with time to play and explore and be back by teatime at 4 pm. It's strange I rarely wore a watch but we knew what time it was, maybe by the height of the sun? We also went to Lilstock beach which is West of Hinckley Point and we had to go across the wheat or cornfields to get there, carefully picking our way around the edges or between the corn, we never wanted to damage the crops so were carefully picking our route through the golden corn sheaves. The pathway to the beach was often difficult to manoeuvre, it was steep and rugged, we remember being careful in our sandals on the rocks. It was always better when the tide was out, as we loved the sand in preference to the rocks and shale.

Pixies Land

Once a remote Bronze Age burial near the coastline stood, covered in a couple of trees; surrounded by pasture, now stands within the complex arena of the Hinckley Point nuclear plants. You used to be able to visit this site but now it is within the grounds of the new constructions.

This was accessible in our time in Somerset, but now is within the greater intricacy of the new Nuclear Plant that is being constructed, so I am not sure if anyone can approach this site now but it is very interesting.

The Pixie's Mound is a Bronze Age round barrow that was excavated in 1907 to show it's the burial site for a few people, there were several beakers and roman objects found in the site. The site is near the village of Wick on the Wick Moor and is said to be the place where the Pixies live. The Pixies are seen to be dressed in red caps and are known locally. It has been known to be bad luck to dig on the land or near the mound and local people feared the Pixie folk. It's easy to imagine little pixies sitting on the mound. Locally the pixies are known for leading people off in the wrong direction or stopping them for getting somewhere they call this Pixie led, for example, if I was going to Bridgwater from Holford but stopped off in Cannington and never continued on to Bridgwater I would have been Pixie Led by not following through with my intentions. Pixies are known to be mischievous at the best of times like fairies they can play tricks on us humble folk.

Pixie Song

"Come to thy copper mine
Come with me
To hear my secrets of long ago

Come see my thresher in the barn
To see how we enchant our corn
Come to the orchard
Come sing we me
Come to the shore,
Come to the shore,
Take by boat by the oar.
Come to the sea, Come to the sea "

By Kim Ora Rose

Pixies are part of the Southwest lands, often known in Somerset, Devon and Cornwall, they are part of our myths and legends. They live in the ancient underground site, the stone circles, ringforts, and barrows. There are many myths about them in Somerset they are often in green outfits with pointed hats, they are mischievous and playful.

At Dodington there is a copper mine, it was mined from late 1500s on and off until the 1800s the engine shafts are still in the field. The ore was rich and copper was exported from Combwich wharf to Swansea, there are several different minerals found in the ground – azurite, calcite, malachite, baryte, chalcocite, graphite and limonite ***.

I love malachite crystals they are very powerful stones for dowsing, ceremony and for vision quests.

Mary Magdalene

The ancient village of Stockland Bristol stands between the marshlands and ancient waterways, between the Steart Peninsula, a village of the marshlands itself. Recorded as Stocheland in the Domesday book meaning a stockade with land and the Bristol part of its name was added much later. This was a village that stood between the waterways a mystical land of ever-flowing water to and fro. The village has iron age origins and is situated inland on dry land, further to the East once stood the bronze age trading villages on the marsh. Within this tiny hamlet is a church dedicated to Mary Magdalene, it was built in 1865 on the place where the 14th-century church to All Saints once stood, the Daniel family of Stockland Manor built the new church which was designed by Mr. Arthur of Plymouth in the old style incorporating some of the original features; part of the screen, 15th-century font, original bells, and Elizabethan cup.

The stone was blue lias rubble was quarried locally in Somerset, it is recognisable and iconic for buildings, especially for manor houses and churches. With its beautiful blue, limestone colours that you will recognise from buildings in Somerset towns like Street and Somerton. This unique stone was formed in the Jurassic period created by layers of shale, limestone, fossils, and is full of iron. It is similar to the rocks and stones found at Kilve and Lilstock beaches and all along the coastline. If you were to visit this part of Somerset you would find many buildings built with this stone.

The manor of Stockland was mentioned in the Domesday book with Ralph de Reuilly from Ralph Pagnell in 1086 and descended to the Maurice de Gaunt who left it in his will a hospital in Bristol, later it was owned by the Bristol Corporation who changed the name of the village and manor house. Thomas Daniel bought the manor back from the corporation and built the existing manor house in 1860. He was wealthy from selling sugar in Bristol and a very powerful family, they rebuilt the manor house and church. After Thomas Daniel's death, the house was passed down in his family to Henry Cave Daniel who sold off the estate after the second world war. The house was divided into three parts it is a listed property being built from blue lias rubble, bath stone with a slate roof in a gothic style. The Daniel family earned their money from the slave trade. Their family had left the area when we lived nearby but these properties remain, I am hoping that by dedicating the church to Mary Magdalene they found some salvation after making their wealth out of slavery. I am not sure why I was writing about Stockland Bristol but it seemed to call to me, or Mary Magdalene. She is often in my writing she guides to share aspects of myself and my spiritual teachings.

Tally Ho!

The local area of Holford is featured in the film The Belstone Fox 1973 with locals stepping in as extras. This is a film about a fox and its life. I have memories of the fox hunting when living at Woodlands, once the hunt ran all over the garden, out of nowhere, there they were in their red coats on horse galloping over our garden chasing the fox. Strangely my mother loved to see the hunt, I think this related to the hunting community around where she lived as a child, but on that day she was not pleased with them at all; to see the riders of the hunt chasing all over our lawn and rose gardens. I can even visualize it now all the riders in their red coats, riding all over or neat lawn, ripping up rose bushes and plants, horses shoe prints all over the garden until they all jumped over the hedgerow into the surrounding fields. Tally Ho! or Not! as the case may be. It is a sport that I am so pleased was banned, whilst the fox is a sly brutal animal the hunt was a cruel sport at any time!

There are other memories of animals that gave us a fright from time to time, sadly our beautiful dogs were poisoned by rat poison in the lane this was very tragic and sad. I had a fright when the pig got out and was in the lane, I was trying to walk to school but it terrified me, and running and crying back home, just to be scolded. I smile looking back at the memory I must have been five or six years old, all dressed in my school uniform with tunic, blazer and straw hat and the pig was large, in my mind she nearly filled the narrow lane, and to be afraid of the pig is strange. Must have been her size and long snout. Pigs can be up to six foot long and they can be strong and heavy too.

There was a time when there was a Billy goat running around our garden too. As I recall this vague memory I think he chased my sister in the garden, she was two years younger than me, he must have lived at the nearby farm, for it wasnt an animal that we had. I am sure he was whitey/gray with horns too.

We used to walk down to the another house down Corewell lane, past the turning upto the main road, to a house on the left, they lady that lived their would drive to Bridgwater for her work or to take her children to school and we would catch a lift with her. We went to St Margarets a private school on the edge of Bridgwater when we lived at Woodlands, before that I think we may have gone to the school at Stogursey for a term or too, I don't have any memories there. At St Margarets I remember having bottles of milk with a nap afterwards, this might have been after lunch. My sister and I have shared memories of eating fish for lunch and being sick later, which put us both of fish for years. Its strange how we share this same memory. We used to go on the school bus home with other children from the villages, I also remember it was a long journey and recall wanting the loo, but it was about an hours drive from school to the drop off under the Woodlands hills, so memories of crossing and recrossing my legs until our stop. Sometimes mum would greet us and help us cross over the main road or other times a lady from the village that used to help mum. Either way we used to skip and sing all the way down the lane to homeward bound. Sometimes picking wild flowers, sometimes chasing butterflies or merrily enjoying the country walk.

Romantic Poets

Not far from Stogursey and Holford is the ancient byway village of Nether Stowey, the main A39 between Bridgwater and Minehead, skirts around the old village, as you reach the village the Medieval red sandstone church stands on your right, next to a creamery farm and to your left is the road into the village. The village dates back to Saxon times and the main road was a military road linking the estates. It is mentioned in the Domesday book with four separate manors that make up this one village.

It's a busy village, and is where my Aunty Pauline lived, she was my mother's sister and she moved to live in Nether Stowey with her husband during the time we lived there. When we moved away to the Midlands we would regularly visit her and I would often stay with her during school holidays. The village consists of older buildings and newer estates akin to other nearby villages, it is famous for its links with Samuel Taylor Coleridge and William Wordsworth the romantic poets.

St Mary's Church stands by Stowey Court at the bottom of Nether Stowey, now cut off from the rest of the village by the A39 bypass that was built in 1968. That must have been built when I lived nearby at Holford and must have changed the journey to and fro to Cannington and Bridgwater where I went to school.

At the top of the hill is Castle Mount I recall going up there on walks, looking over the countryside below, only a few stones remain from the 11th century Motte and Bailey castle. Near the castle, there used to be a small chapel dedicated to St Michael. From the top of the mount, you can see across to Hinkley Point, to the Welsh coast, and the Quantock hills. The castle fell into ruin sometime in the 15th century. It had been constructed as a fortress, with its Norman keep, with walls some six feet deep. The site was used during later centuries for fighting and entertainment.

The houses in Lime Street and Castle Street are very old, some of them from medieval times, there is a small brook or stream that runs down Castle Street and I remember playing something like "Pooh sticks" watching twigs and sticks flow as a child.

Nether Stowey is the village that the poet Coleridge lived in in 1795 for three years where he wrote several famous poems. He lived near the top of Lime Street as seen on this map, this house is now a museum owned by the National Trust. Nether Stowey once had a castle similar to Stogursey, built to defend the coast, now a ruin on Castle Hill. My Aunty lived just off Castle Street and I used to stay with her during my early teens. I remember going horse-riding from the village and going on lots of walks in the country lanes.

We stayed in Lime Street in a cottage in May 2020 the houses were built in the 1700s and are in a strange overlapping design, the inside of the house does not reflect the size of the yard behind, and bedrooms sit over the next-door dwelling, they are terraced and no doubt the ownership boundaries have shifted over time.

Fairy Realms

My mother and I used to love flower fairies, only recently my father gave me her small book on the flower fairies and this felt so perfect, so special like she is watching down from heaven guiding my father to give me this book, it is tiny but one of the most precious gifts I have been given. So many memories flood back of how we loved collecting the flower fairy porcelain plates and used to have them up in our kitchen, this must have been in my late teens so in the early 1980s. Mum used to collect small china flower ornaments and there are a few still at my dad's house this is another way my mother bought flowers into her home, in ornaments and she always had fresh flowers every week in our hallway. So every time you walked through the hall between rooms you were receiving the glowing light of the flowers. As I write I have roses, tulips, and daffodils in my home and they certainly bring some light into the days of winter. We have been reorganising our pots in the garden to bring all the spring flowers to the front to enjoy as the bulbs are emerging.

Spring is my favourite time of year not only are the flowers coming back to life, but I too awaken from my winter resting and start to look forward to the warmer days. Flower fairies have probably been around forever and they have bought delight and wonder to adults and children. I remember seeing a fairy when I was with my friend on Shell Island, it was so marvellous to see one, just at twilight, so magical and although I've seen them at other times this was so special.

Cicely Mary Barker created her Flower Fairies with her drawings of flowers and fairies which she based on real children from a nearby nursery school. They really bring the fairies to life. I believe she created 170 drawings in total and these were some of the images on the china plates we had at home and within the tiny book, my father gave me. This little book has drawings and poems and they so delight me, for in this book there are poems and flower guardians and there are images too some photographs and some of my paintings and illustrations. Cicely Mary Barker was born in West Croydon in 1895 that was the same year that one of my grandfathers was born, my mother's father Walter Osborne he was born in Burton upon Trent, my hometown. Walter was the son of a baker and one of his loves was horses, this love of horses runs through our family. He also enjoyed growing vegetables and flowers in this garden.

According to Cicely Mary Barker, the flowers fairies were tiny creatures that were only 20cm tall and they lived with the flowers and whenever a seed sprouted then a flower fairy was born. How magical is this? Each of the flower fairies had a role to play in looking after the flowers as they grow. I simply love this idea of their role; my Guardians are so much an integral part of the flower's life too. My daughter asked me for some ideas for my birthday and I said just one day ago I would like something with the Flower Fairies, then behold, the universe returned with this tiny book that belonged to my mother, how wonderful that was to receive. I cannot tell how much it means to me to hold in my hands a book that belonged to me about flowers and their fairies. It's a tiny book but so special. I know she is watching down over me and hearing that request and answer from my daughter about what would I like? Sometimes you receive just what you asked for so ask for something you would really like? You never know who is listening to your conversations and this leads me to my abundance of teachings. Focus more on what you would like in your life rather than what you don't want.

Bringing this back to Cicely, she was ill as a child and it didn't stop her from being a successful artist and her drawings are enjoyed today over hundred years after her birth. She lived a rich life with her artwork until 1973.

Cicely wrote in the foreword to Flower Fairies of the Wayside, 'So let me say quite plainly, that I have drawn all the plants and flowers very carefully, from real ones; and everything that I have said about them is as true as I could make it. But I have never seen a fairy; the fairies and all about them are just "pretend".

I love to read her poems and look upon her drawings and paintings, to me the fairies are real, just as real as you and me, I hope she is listening, as I say these words and now she is in heaven she knows that they are real. I see fairies, in my mind, in the hedgerows, in my heart, I see my Guardians of the flowers in the same way. Being a channeller of light probably helps, yet you too will feel their energies as you open up to sense them. Maybe you can see them too if you open your awareness and your imagination to sense them for yourself.

The Song of The May Fairy
My buds, they cluster small and green;
The sunshine gaineth heat;
Soon shall the hawthorn tree be clothed
As with a snowy sheet

O magic sight, the hedge is white,
My scent is very sweet;
And lo, where I am come indeed,
The Spring and Summer meet.

CMB

All change....

We moved to the Midlands in the spring of 1970 and at first, this was a rude awakening, my father had started a new job and we couldn't find a suitable house straight away, so we lived in a tiny miner's cottage near Ibstock with no garden, just a yard for a few months until we found our forever home in the summertime. I have many dark memories from this time, after leaving the deep countryside we lived next to a major road and the coal lorries would trundle past our home day and night as this was at the height of the colliery industry nearby. We used to see shapes in the curtains, shadows on the walls from the traffic outside or something else I can not tell. We went to the local school which seemed old even then it had been built in the Victorian times, it was small, we share a classroom with another year group. My only memories are walking to school again along the road and by some grassy ground. There is a school photo of me there, that was always in my grandfather's china cabinet, I was smiling so I must have been happy there.

This was something quite new to us, our life in Somerset had been full of tractors and sounds of the countryside, of baling hay, looking after orphaned sheep and chasing piglets.

Finally in the early summer we moved to our "forever home" in Burton upon Trent, our new home was an Edwardian house on the Northeast end of the town, overlooking the river, it was spacious with five bedrooms, a large garden and it became our new home. It is there many of my new memories connecting to the garden and nearby countryside formed. We had a large front garden, elevated from the road, and a large two-tiered back garden which evolved over the years. We now lived on a street of Victorian and Edwardian-styled houses which had been built to accommodate the managers and workers of the breweries.

Our particular house used to be owned by a family called Rowland they were surveyors and auctioneers they lived in the home during WW1 and their daughters lived in the house sometime before it changed hands and we later bought the house. It was built at the turn of the century with many features from the Victorian Era, will tall ceilings, fireplaces, servants bells still exist but the hired hands have long departed. We used to love to ring the bells from different rooms, I wonder now as I write if there are any left? There used to be one in my parents' bedroom, in the lounge and front (drawing) rooms, reminding of the traditional formal names, the Master Bedroom, the Drawing Room, we still have dining rooms today but how many of us have Drawing Rooms and Morning Rooms? I am currently in this lockdown like to use my dining room as a morning, writing room, it is where I am writing this book, then to retire to the "lounge". Can you imagine lying in bed ringing the bell for the maid? What fun! I am sure there are a few people we know that would love such a thing, now we can text our family to bring us a coffee or breakfast in bed. What fun!

The bell had exactly the same ring sound as the front door, come to think about just that, it was probably the same bell system. Well, we used to ring the bell in one room, when my Mum went to the door we would hide and run off to be outside or somewhere else when she would say "Who rang the Bell?" we were little "terrors" that's for sure. As I am sure most children are!

Our house and many others were originally mainly breweries in the town that merged and became four main ones when we arrived in 1970. When I was researching my family tree you could see all the brewery managers on the Censuses and where they lived. My Grandfather loved researching history, maybe that's where my love of history first stemmed from, he researched his own family tree over years of research. Without the internet or microfiches in the library, that's where I started over twenty years ago. He would go to Somerset House to find all the old records and trace his family name back in time. Through the parish records and censuses and it's a fascinating journey. It was grandfather that researched our house's history, he just to take me to the Museum to see the photographs of Mr Rowland that lived in our house, he had been Mayor and his photo was in there. Not sure if that photo exists now for the Museum was closed down so many years ago. We had a fascinating fireplace in our "drawing room" the top had was dated but was much older than the elaborate bottom section. We never really found out where it had come from probably to do with the Rowland's.

Being a sensitive child when we first moved to this new home, it was quite different from our previous homes, it was colder, for we never had open fires, as I am writing this, I pause did we? I am beginning to wonder about the heating, we had gas fires in individual rooms and a coal-fired boiler in the kitchen this heated the water and the room. We might have had an open fire, just can't remember, and why it could be important now fifty years later I do not know. But it was colder than our house in Somerset. It was bigger and you would do well to keep the individual doors closed or you might lose all the heat out into the double-height hallway. Come to think about it I think it might have been colder in the 1970s there were stories about the mini Ice Ace so it might not have been the fault of the heating in the house at all. I remember complaining about the house being cold to my Dad and getting a lecture on how much it costs to heat as it was. Days before insulation I am sure. We just wore layers and layers and layers lay on our beds, do you remember how you would have sheets, blankets, counterpanes all tucked in tight to keep us warm whilst the icicles decorate the windowpanes. Such memories make me smile. We survived and lived to tell the tale.

You might ask were there any ghosts in your home? This question might have never occurred to you but I am not sure, there were creaking noises at night and later I did find out that one of the previous occupants had died on the WW1 battlefields, I do remember finding some of the rooms eerie and there was sometimes a small boy with us when we were children. I clearly remember him as I type, he was about six or seven years old and was always in shorts, no matter what the weather. I can see him now playing around the apple tree seat, I am not sure if he was real or in spirit.

In the 1970s town was still dominated by the breweries with the railway lines running all over the town, across roads connecting the breweries with their buildings and logistics. I am still living in this town some 50 years later and whilst my heart remembers my childhood home in Somerset it is firmly rooted in Staffordshire. The town has changed so much over the last thirty years or so after then took a lot of the old railway lines away and the brewing process changed. Whilst it is still an industrial town with its history full of brewing, it still has parts of the old Abbey.

For me I love the River Trent, the washlands, with its many walks along the river, these are where my heart yearns to walk amongst the willow trees, watch and wait for the call of the heron, listening for the kingfisher and seeing the majestic swans on the river. I often think that without the river it would be a dull place to live and whilst we are miles and miles from the sea, we do have the river and it is so magical. There are so many walks along the river in different directions South along the Westerly banks towards Walton on Trent, I like to start from the Riverside Inn, and walk south, along the banks of the river, this was once fields but not full of trees, lots of newly planted trees line the banks of the river, you will find the Peace Garden there on many a pleasant evening, I love to walk at near sunset and see how the redden sky lights up the sky.

You can walk in a Northerly direction from the Riverside Inn Garden's and walk by the side of the Banks of the river sandwiched by the Cherry Trees and golf course, this is another favourite walk of mine, especially in spring when the trees are in full blossom. These are just a couple of lovely walks there are so many more plus the numerous walks along the canal which reminds you of the industrial past when they would have been one of the main waterways to connect to the sea. Full of barges laden with beer kegs and heavy loads traveling up and down the waterways to Manchester and beyond for Indian shores bound.

There are some very special places in the town, the Abbey which is now a restaurant and the St Modwen's Church which has some fascinating stories. The Abbey had been large and important before the dissolution of the Abbeys and Monasteries it was located by the River Trent too, before the breweries this was an important town for trade, there was a weekly market and annual fair.

Waterloo Water Tower stands high above the town on the Northeast, with its Victorian brick tower, that you can see for miles and miles. We lived below the water tower and whenever we were coming home we would look out for it as a landmark to know that we were nearly home. It stands high up at the end of Tower Road beside a trackway which runs down to the cemetery next to a small woodland known as Waterloo Clump this was planted to commemorate the Duke of Wellington's victory in 1815. The tower is over 24m high built on a concrete base with brickwork. At the top the tower is castellated, inside the tower there is a cast-iron water tank, the water was pumped up to the tower to provide water pressure to the homes in Winshill.

In the past before Ashby Road had been built this was the road up towards Ashby from the town, now a narrow track. The old drover's way, that now has been almost forgotten as it nestles within between the gardens and fields yet shows the times of yesteryear.

As we had moved from one county to another our playground was still the fields, now up to the tower and beyond over the fields and wherever our hearts desired for still in those times gone by there were links by green land to almost everywhere. Such is life in our forever green England.

Joining the Dots

As I am bringing my childhood to life again through these memories everything in my past is so relevant in my present, as our lives shape us into who we are.

In my early years, I loved history, the wildness of the countryside, and knowing who had walked over this land before. I love the land, its vibration, its energy, its hidden paths, mysteries, and as I walk on the secrets open up to me one by one. I love the springs, brooks, and waterways that connect the land with their ever-flowing joy of water, life-giving water that feeds our soul. I loved the spirit guardians, the flower fairies, and the little folk I love their music, their songs too.

Looking up at the sky seeing it for the first time and knowing that generations of people have looked up and seen the sky too, in all its colours, moods, and wonder. We can hardly see the night sky from where I live now, but if you went back 200 years the night sky would have been so clear and it was full of wonder, it is still there beyond the town's lighting systems. Sometimes we need to look beyond what we are seeing and seek the inner vision; this can be internally inside ourselves or in our external physical world. There is so much that we do not understand and so much we are trying to remember from our other lives. Everything has a consciousness, all beings, all life, animals, birds, insects, plant life, etc. Even when it has been transformed eg a tree cut down to make a chair it still holds the essence of the consciousness of the whole tree. This is why we often choose different materials for our furniture or ornaments.

I love wood, I like it varnished, carved, painted or natural, behind my house there is a small woodland and where I lived in Somerset our home was called Woodlands, later when we moved to the Midlands we had planted trees in our garden and there were other giants that grew beyond our garden wall. I was never sure about being a "tree hugger" but when I do hug a tree, wow the feeling is wonderful, I remember hugging the giant Yew trees in the Chalice Well Gardens in Glastonbury last year with my husband. We had gone to be part of the global anchoring of the light on Glastonbury Tor in August, this was the last Sunday with Amanda Lorence. I had been tuning in her weekly anchoring of light on the Tor for weeks, and this was to be the final one. So, my husband and I made the journey to Glastonbury from the Midlands, we met some wonderful people there. Amanda has such a wonderful worldwide following and it was so good to meet like-minded Souls who were drawn to be there too. After the gathering on the Tor, we had lunch then went to visit the Chalice Wells, it was raining so we sheltered in an arbour looking at the giant yews and later hugged them.

So much magic jumps out when you hug trees, so much wonder and messages of hope and endurance for trees witness so much. Those in the Chalice Wells see so many pilgrims that come to visit the gardens in awe and wonder and they stand to witness and support the garden from the many visitors. There I am standing under the trees, they are damp from the drizzling rain, droplets falling around me as I hug the expansive tree trunks, how old are these trees? I do not know, but they hold so much "joy" I totally recommend you hug trees. Try it out for yourself. I often go on walks in woodlands, forests, and by the river. The river is strewn with Willow Trees there is more than one variety. The flowers and trees are entwined as in nature, that was how they wished to be presented in this body of writing.

Yew Trees at Chalice Well, Glastonbury
Photograph by Kim Ora Rose 2020

Joys of the Garden

It was as if most of my childhood was spent out of doors, in the garden, over the fields, in the woods, wherever I lived it was the outdoors I loved. I have so few memories of the indoor places or the rooms and so many of the outside places. Of flower beds, trees, collecting conkers in the woods and pinecones, pinching pea pods, and trying to boil potatoes in our den. Of hiding in the neighbour's garden whilst we were scrumming trying desperately not to get caught. Memories of climbing over garden fences to reach new friends and explore each other's outdoor spaces. The one real benefit of moving to the Midlands was that we had more friends than lived nearby and this was an enormous plus. There were other families with children our ages and we played with so many of them.

My mother loved roses and filled large rose beds with deep crimson red roses, there were lots of wildflowers growing in the hedgerows and other flowers in the garden. My childhood was spent in the gardens ours and other peoples, or in the nearby fields, even when we moved we were not far from footpaths and fields there is so much of my going up years that were spent in nature.

We had roses at Calvi our first home overlooking the churchyard, roses at Woodlands, and more roses at Hamilton House, my mother loved roses, always red, she loved red roses. We did have pink Rosa ones a little like wild ones on our back garden but her favourites were always red. The ones she planted over thirty years ago are still blooming now. There had been red roses planted soon after we arrive in Burton Upon Trent and these were the second bed of roses called my Dad tells me they are called "Ena Harkness" he is so proud of them and remembers their name. This rose is often bought as a climbing rose but ours were definitely shrubs they did grow tall and flowered every year. When I researched this rose I found that it was one from a family of rose breeders called Harkness who started their business in 1879, in Yorkshire by two brothers John and Robert Harkness and they had many varieties of roses. When they started their business Queen Victoria bought roses from them. The climate in Yorkshire was not good for their business so they moved to Hertfordshire for a warmer climate in 1892. Two of their favourite roses were "Frensham" and "Ena Harkness" these were both introduced in 1946. Another interesting snippet I discovered was that the Poet Ted Hughes worked at the nursery in 1955 and this reminds me that I used to read his poems in my late teenage years and how I love poetry. So much in this journey with the flowers bring me home to poetry and the inspiration of words.

The Rosa variety in my mother's garden reminds me of some wild roses I saw in Provence, Southern France growing in the wild places with their delicate but hardy soft rose petals and spiky thorns. We saw lots of these on soft pink roses when we were searching for the Source of the River Huveanue (Les Sources de l'Huveaune), strangely we never found it, but it is truly beautiful. Apparently, people on the Mary Magdalene Pilgrimages go to visit this river, and a photographer shared photos of the area and this sparked off a delude of visitors, who were turning up in droves to photograph the river. The local council closed off the area, banned parking, and gave out fines for any cars parked nearby. Such as where it had been easy to find the signs had been removed and whilst we had a wonderful walk in the wild countryside in baking heat, we didn't find it this time. Maybe next time. The walk was full of wildflowers and maybe that was what I was meant to find.

The wild roses grow in the hedges on the pasture lands near the village of Combwich in Somerset in the softest pink, the colour of Mary Magdalene's bliss.

It was much later in her life that my mother began to love pink roses, in those few years before she died she loved them with cherubs and the deepest blue she was a true Magdalene sister of the rose, probably always but most definitely in those last few years when she found more peace within herself than ever before. Mum had always loved Blues, she was the first person I know to decorate her "living room" in blue, most of the other families I knew were decorating in greens and browns, so blue was so "out there", she had blue hessian walls and white on the others with painted floorboards and Turkish rugs, with Hollywood photographs. It was so dramatic in white, blue, and black, very visionary or so it seemed. Later it was decorated in softer pinks and blues with roses and cherubs.

My mother was a beautiful Soul she suffered from depressions with highs and lows and yet she was charismatic and full of life and light. She loved roses and filled large rose beds with deep crimson red roses, there were lots of wildflowers growing in the hedgerows and other flowers in the garden. My childhood was spent in the gardens ours and other peoples, or in the nearby fields, even when we moved we were not far from footpaths and fields there is so much of my going up years that were spent in nature.

We had roses at Calvi our first home overlooking the churchyard, roses at Woodlands, and more roses at Hamilton House, my mother loved roses, always red. Red was a colour she really identified with and one that I never did really. It's the colour of Love, the colour the root chakra of passion and of fire. She did possess an abundance of life and life in her heart and maybe this is why she loved Red so much. At our "Forever Home," we had a large rear garden full of daisy perennials and many other flowers in the garden, our house was always full of flowers, my mother loved flowers and she has given me the gift of loving flowers too.

In those early years, the garden was a bit of a jungle with white rockery stones, old pathways from the days before, and an old apple tree stood in the upper garden with a wooden seat around it. I have a fondness for orchards and apple trees, especially the apple blossom, not from this garden but from a life long ago, past life or time before. Often in meditation, I will slip off to the orchards, amongst the low growing apple and pear trees, in the blossom, and in the full height of harvest when the apples are collected. This has been one of my favourite places to centre my energy amongst the orchard full of trees, with all the scents of the bountiful apples to absorb all their many gifts of wisdom, eternal life, and rebirth.

As a child, I was always inquisitive I have so many memories of collecting the rose petals to make rose water, trying to make rose perfumes I remember not having anything special just the things in our kitchen so collecting roses petals in a colander and washing them under the tap, more ended up being eaten than used in the rose water. Which I stored in jam jars. I loved their velvety sweet petals and heavenly perfumes. It's so difficult to pass a rose smelling its sweet perfume. We coated petals in egg whites and dipped them in sugar these were so delicious and one of favourite ways to decorate a cake.

There are so many memories of eating flowers and plants in the garden, it's a wonder I didn't get ill, but must have instinctively known which were poisonous. One of my favourites was eating the leaves of the mint plant, never knowing how many different mint plants there were, we only had one the spearmint variety I now have at least three different varieties in my garden including peppermint, apple mint, and catmint. I use them in salads and recipes and our rabbits love nibbling the aromatic leaves too. In contrast to my childhood garden mine is small, triangular in shape, and has many areas that are in the dappled shade so it has been difficult to make the most of this garden, however, it is in recent years that I have discovered the best flowers to grow where and some have really taken over the garden.

So many memories of playing in our garden, over the wall, over other gardens and into the wildness of the fields and woodlands. As a child I would talk to the flowers, trees, and animals and would hear them talk to me, I was always a sensitive child and the flower spirits were my constant companions. I spent many an hour lost in thought with my constant friends some in this realm and some in others, always surrounded by ancestors and visitors from one dimension to another. My reality of life was different to others, I was " off with the fairies" in the most literal of meanings, off in another dimension that bought so much joy to my life. Even now as an adult I have moments, hours even, journeying in other realms with my guides and companions to another place in time.

Believe in magic, never give up on it
Listen to the magic as it spins on the air
As a thousand leaves fall of an autumn day
Fill your cup of golden mead
Believe in fairy folk as they believe in you!

by Kim Ora Rose

Always Flowers

My love of flowers has been like a constant journey my favourite flower was a white lily, I had them in my wedding bouquet with pink roses and soft blue flowers. So many years later I discovered that white lilies were the flower of the priestess and its makes sense to me know.

My mother loved horses and ponies, her father had kept horses for his father's business to pull the baker's wagon and he was responsible for breaking them in and training them. She instilled this love of horses in us from an early age. Mum had her own natural remedies to use in the home, she always used a witch hazel lotion for her skin, even later when she had more money to spend, she still chose to use witch hazel as a cleanser for treating any blemishes and she had the most perfect of skins.
She used to make lavender bags of dried flowers in muslin bags to hand in her bedroom and I remember that musky scent on her clothes. She was a very talented seamstress she could make anything with fabric I shall write about this more in a later chapter.

Flowers, herbs, and trees always bring me home to me, to my core being, with their subtle energies and power. Remembering my favorites from my childhood take me straight back to the narrow lanes and abundance fields of West Somerset, to the field so gold and blue, to the magic of every turn of the lane. Flowers have their own vibration and they are such healers, they bring their upliftment with each flower. My mother loved flowers, she loved to have them in her gardens, in her home and she loved roses until the day she passed. During her life, she had bouts of depression throughout her life, when we were children she received very aggressive treatment and I think she tried to avoid ever going back to those depths. She found natural ways to control her moods and lift her spirits and flowers were part of that. I guess today you would say she had bipolar and there might be more helpful for her condition that was less aggressive than that she experienced in 1964. One of her ways was to always have the house full of flowers and although she never spoke about her low moods, her garden and flowers were very important to her. She loved all flowers and kept them in her hallway so you walk past them many times a day and feel their uplifting energies. She would have new flowers every Friday and they would keep flowering for the whole week through, filling the house with their vibration, exquisite scents, and glorious colours.

In memory of my Mother and her gardens of beautiful flowers

Appendices

Jurassic Rocks & Quantock Stone
Churches

Jurassic rocks and Quantock stone

Blue Anchor to Lilstock has been recognised as a geological site of special scientific interest since 1971, the beaches within include Blue Anchor, Kilve, East Quantockhead, Lilstock and Stofold.

Kilve Beach

Kilve village is set on the A39 between Bridgwater and Minehead, about halfway between the two, it is a few miles from Holford. It's a fascinating beach for the fossil hunter. There is a unique specimen of an ichthyosaur that was found on the beach. This is a fabulous stretch of coast full of interest, with limestone cliffs, slate and shingle layers and sweeping rock formations.

Kilve beach is within the Blue Anchor Bay to Steart Peninsula SSI protected area and is one of the beaches where you might find fossils, the beach is layered in rocks and stones, there are some rock pools when the tide is out too. It is the home of the Blue Ben Dragon's skull that was found of a fossilised ichthyosaur that is on display in a local museum.

Stofold Beach

This is a small beach near Hinckley Point, it has part of the Jurassic coastline with shingle, pebbles, limestone and shale. In 2019 another ichthyosaur skeleton was found in the mud. It is a beach where you can find fossils too. These coastal places provide examples of early Jurassic stages in their faults filled with fossils, ammonites, shells, and fish remains.

Triscombe Stone

This refers to a small standing stone that can be found on the

Quantock Hills is dates back to the Bronze age and was a meeting place on the old drovers' road along the top of the hills. There are superstitions that if you sit on it, you may be granted a wish. The name "Tris" refers to a Celtic word for "meeting" and "combe" comes from the Saxon word for a steep narrow valley or large hollow on the side of a hill. Triscombe means a meeting place on a steep hill. There is a car park situated near Triscombe Stone and this road leads past the quarry and down to the Blue Ball Inn into the quaint village of Triscombe. The stone was a meeting place for lovers too.

Triscombe quarry

The quarry at Triscombe is now closed down, but it was a busy quarry just up from the Blue Ball public house, the road was closed when I last went there, but open for hikers. The quarry was on the largest on the Quantocks for the red sandstone called Hangman's Grit, it was heavily quarried and leaves its mark on the landscape. Many of the local buildings were made out of this red stone. The village of Triscombe lies near West Bagborough and Crowcombe on the Quantock hills. It is a small village with a few houses. The quarry was closed in 1999 and the land is now returning to be natural habitat. The Hangman's Gritstone are hard rocks that were formed some 500 million years ago. The quarry probably dates back to the Bronze Age, as there were many cairns and forts dating back to the Bronze and Iron Age built on the Quantock hills.The red sandstone outcrops were first quarried in early 14th century, there is evidence of its many uses locally in the churches and buildings. Holford Church, West Bagbourgh Church and Crowcombe church as many others locally were built with the red sandstone blocks from the Triscombe quarry. The quarry was only a few miles over the hills and a perfect stone for the church.

Blue lais rough stone

As mentioned at Stockland Bristol, this was the name stone used for the St Mary Magdalene Church built in 1860, it is a natural Somerset stone made from nearby quarries, the stone comprised of shale, iron-rich mud, and limestone, similar to the rocks on the North-Western shoreline, good examples can be seen at Kilve beach. The stone comes from the Jurassic period and is filled with fossils. It is the stone used for the rebuilding of the Stockland Manor house by Thomas Daniel too and many other churches and houses in Somerset. There are several quarries in Somerset with Blue Lais stone that is still used today.

Churches

There are several interesting churches in and around the Quantock Hills many that were part of our childhood.

Crowcombe – The Church of the Holy Ghost

The church was built in the Quantocks red sandstone, Hangman's Grit from the Triscombe quarry, with a slate roof, the earliest part was built in the 14th century. The tower dates back to the 14th century and the rest of the building is later. There was another church on this site dating back to Saxon times. The north chapel was used by the family at the manor house at Crowcombe Court. There are links to the green man and pagan life craved onto the bench ends with the two-headed dragon too. In the churchyard, there is a large medieval cross. The village of Crowcombe lies at the foot of a combe, above the village is a higher ground called Hangman Grits, where are large areas of a sandstone quarry.

Dodington – All Saints Church

This church is in the small hamlet of Corewell, near Holford, this is a Grade I listed building and belongs to the parish of Holford.

Its was originally built in the 12th century but has been modified over the centuries. It is next to Dodington Hall. The church has been expanded in the 15th century and again in the 16th and 19th centuries. It has been built in the local red sandstone and parts are rendered in white, now patchy. Within the church are a Jacobean-style altar, Victorian pulpit, and Gothic lectern. There are traces of painting from the medieval periods too. It is an interesting church, I don't remember going inside this church but it was only a mile or so from our home at Woodlands, we would have walked by it often.

Next door is Dodington Hall which was built in the 15th century, replacing a previous building. The house was built in the local red sandstone with a slate roof and tall chimneys. The manor house was extended in the late 1500s but left to be a farmhouse in the 17th century. (Source: https://www.visitchurches.org.uk/visit/church-listing/all-saints-dodington.html)

*Dodington Hall Postcard by **Old Postcard by Montague Cooper Postmark Clevedon 1908***

Holford – St Mary the Virgin

As with many of the local churches this church is dedicated to the Virgin Mary. The church is built with the local red sandstone from Hangman Grit quarry at Triscombe in the 1300s. There was a previous place of worship on the land before this church was built. This is a small church near where I used to live.

Kilve- Church of St Mary

This church dates back to the 14th century, it is a small church that depicts the size of the community. The tower has had a lot of restorative work done and the whole church is rendered in a shade of white. The building was built with blue lias stone. Next to the church is the ruins of the Chantry which is attached to some houses and a tea garden operates next to the ruins. The Chantry was founded in 1329 when five monks lived there, their founder was Simon de Furneaux. The building fell in ruin before the dissolution of the monasteries and was used as a barn for many years. There are stories about smugglers that frequented the dangerous Kilve beach where many a ship was wrecked on the shale stones.

It is situated near the beach carpark and there is a good circular walk from the beach over the coastal path to the neighbouring village of East Quantockhead and back over the fields to the church.

Nether Stowey – St Mary Church, The Blessed Virgin Mary

Another red sandstone church built in the 14th century, dedicated to Mother Mary, the church of St Mary the Virgin, with its 15th century tower and its expansion in the 1850s, is now a Grade II listed building. Prior to the building of this church, there was an earlier smaller 12th-century church, the parish of Nether Stowey links to the other Quantock villages of Overstowey, Spaxton, Aisholt, Enmore, and Goathurst. It is a striking architectural design with its red sandstone west tower, its buttresses, and pinnacles. The tower holds six bells which were recast in 1914. Strangely the A39 separates the church from the main part of the village, you can see the church next to the Cricketer Farm, just outside of the village with the main A39 road running through.

Stockland Bristol - St Mary Magdalene

Originally a church was built in the 14th century dedicated to All Saints at Stockland Bristol, then later in the eighteen hundred, Thomas Daniel bought the church land, manor house, and other lands at Stockland Bristol and had a new church built. This was newly dedicated to Saint Mary Magdalene in the 14th-century style in local stone. This was a fitting tribute to the small village that edges up to the marshlands of the Bristol Channel. I am not sure about him as a man, for his wealth was gained from slavery and sugar plantations in Barbados. I have included this church for is dedicated to Mary Magdalene and the villages close proximity to my home villages. During my time living in West Somerset, the land and manor house had long been sold off and the Daniels had moved away from this area.

Stogursey – St Andrews Church

The Church dates back to the early 12th century, it stands on a corner at the bottom of Church Street, turning into Priory Hill it was built originally as a Benedictine priory church in 1117. It is a Grade 1 listed building; it was built by William de Falaise who was lord of the manor in 1086 and this building incorporated earlier features of another structure. It was expanded in 1180, and when the priory was dissolved in 1440 it became a parish church. As with other churches over the decades, it was altered in 15th century and 19th centuries. The tower holds six bells the oldest being from 1611. (Source: http://stogursey-online.uk/st-andrews-church-stogursey).

Stogursey is one of the largest churches in these ancient villages, its packed with interest and has some interesting features, externally and internally it has been painted in now fading white, with render over the original stone.**

I was baptised at this church and lived opposite it for a few years, when I used to visit my grandfather I would go to Sunday services. My grandfather's ashes are buried in the churchyard amongst the rows of daffodils.

West Bagborough – St Pancras

This church was first built in the 14th century in the red sandstone rock from the Quantock hills, the quarry was very close by to the ancient village of West Bagborough. The church is situated next to Bagborough House. The church was restored and added to in the 1800s when a North aisle was added and further work was done in the early 20th century when aisles and an organ were installed. The church stands higher than the main village, it is a larger church than some of the local places of worship. In the past, the church had been dedicated to The Holy Trinity and I am not sure why it changed its name. St Pancras has a feast day of 12th

May, Sanctus Pancratius was a Roman citizen who converted to Christianity and was apparently beheaded for his faith when he was a teenager. His name means "he who holds everything" he is associated with children, jobs, and health and in London, England there is the St Pancras Railway Station.

This was the spiritual home of my Aunt Mrs. Betty Watson and where I visited on numerous occasions as a child for events and latterly for my aunt's funeral.

The neighbouring Bagborough house was used in the film about Coleridge "Pandemonium" with many local landmarks.

Sources

**Source: https://www.greatenglishchurches.co.uk/html/stogursey.html

*** https://www.mindat.org/loc-1613.html

About The Author

Kim Ora Rose

 Kim was born at Bridgwater, Somerset, and lived in surrounding villages before moving to the Midlands where she lives with her husband and dogs. She is a retired teacher, mystic, energy healer, and writer.

Books By This Author

Unlocking Your Abundance With Mary Magdalane

This book takes you on a journey with Mary Magdalene with her rainbow of sacred roses which guide you through each of your chakras to unlock your blockages and uncover your own potential for unlimited abundance, love, happiness and joy. As you connect with each of the eight roses and their meditations you will open up your energy centers with the loving support and wisdom of Mary Magdalene and Mother Mary. As a Mary Magdalene High Priestess Kim has channeled each of the eight meditations and wisdom through her deep connection to Mary Magdalene which are very powerful. You will receive information on how to download the accompanying MP3 Audios. This book was written after Kim's Pilgrimage to France when she received the Pink Bliss energy initiation at Sainte Baume Magdalene Cave in Provence.

There are eight short meditations that can be downloaded free of charge to accompany this book

Sacred Temple Of The White Flame

White Flame is a unique powerful healing modality that prepares you for ascension and higher personal development. This is a gift from Soul to Soul, it will open you up to unlimited energies from the Sacred Temple of the White Flame.

This unique healing modality was channelled by Kim Ora Rose in 2018 it was through her advanced dedication with Mary

Magdalene that she received the White Flame energies and symbols. It is overseen by the Divine Council of Light, Goddess Isis and her son Horus. Through Kim's spiritual journey as a medium, mystic, healer she channelled white light for healing and creating sacred space. After her advanced dedication with Mary Magdalene and her searching for the truth, she connected with the Divine Council of Light. They are a collective consciousness of multi-dimensional light beings who are supporting the Earth's ascension. White Flame is a "Soul-to-Soul" gift, a healing modality that opens gateways to ancient wisdom from the Egyptian Temples of Isis and Horus. Learning about the ancient symbols and being initiated to the Sacred Temple of the White Flame.

New Dawn: Poems Inspired By The Divine Feminine

These poems reflect a journey home through the divine feminine energies of Mary Magdalene and her "Way of Love" of all humanity. Dipping into the divine feminine energies of intuition, creation, faith, and love project the fullest energies of unity, love, and peace. Through this book, you will engage in the emotions of self-discovery of healing, and awakening. Allow the poems in this book to resonate deeply in your soul, let them empower you as the new dawn emerges in the unity of love.

Printed in Great Britain
by Amazon

85994497R10061